CATHOLICISM
AND
FOLK RELIGION

Other booklets in the Affirming Catholicism series

Affirming Confession
John Davies

Christ in Ten Thousand Places – A Catholic Perspective on Christian Encounter with Other Faiths
Michael Ipgrave

History, Tradition and Change – Church History and the Development of Doctrine
Peter Hinchliff

Imagining Jesus – An Introduction to the Incarnation
Lewis Ayres

'Is the Anglican Church Catholic?' – The Catholicity of Anglicanism
Vincent Strudwick

Lay Presidency at the Eucharist
Benedict Green

'Making Present' – The Practice of Catholic Life and Liturgy
Christopher Irvine

'Permanent, Faithful, Stable' – Christian Same-Sex Partnerships
Jeffrey John

Politics and the Faith Today – Catholic Social Vision for the 1990s
Kenneth Leech

Trinity and Unity
Jane Williams

What is Affirming Catholicism?
Jeffrey John

Why Women Priests? – The Ordination of Women and the Apostolic Ministry
Jonathan Sedgwick

AFFIRMING CATHOLICISM

Jeremy Morris

CATHOLICISM AND FOLK RELIGION

DARTON·LONGMAN + TODD

JEREMY MORRIS is Assistant Curate at St Mary's, Battersea. He read history at Oxford and theology at Cambridge, training for the ministry at Westcott House. Two of his special interests come together in this pamphlet: the history of Anglican Catholicism and the relationship between the Church and society.

Published by Darton, Longman and Todd, 1 Spencer Court,
140–142 Wandsworth High Street, London SW18 4JJ
in association with Affirming Catholicism, St Mary-le-Bow,
Cheapside, London EC2V 6AU

ISBN 0–232–52138–7

Booklets designed by Bet Ayer, phototypeset by Intype, London
and printed by Halstan and Co Ltd, Amersham, Bucks

CONTENTS

Affirming Catholicism

Affirming Catholicism has never been, and is not intended to be, yet another 'party' within the Church of England or the Anglican Communion but rather a movement of encouragement and hope.

A group of lay people and clergy met together in 1990 to identify that authentic Catholic tradition within the Church which appeared to be under threat. Wider support was expressed at a public meeting on 9 June 1990 in London and at a residential conference in York in July 1991.

Since then Affirming Catholicism has been afforded charitable status. The following statement is extracted from the Trust Deed:

> It is the conviction of many that a respect for scholarship and free enquiry has been character-istic of the Church of England and of the Churches of the wider Anglican Communion from earliest times and is fully consistent with the status of those Churches as part of the Holy Catholic Church. It is desired to establish a charitable educational foundation which will be true both to those characteristics and to the Catholic tradition within Anglicanism ... The object of the foundation shall be the advancement of education in the doctrines and the historical development of the Church of England and the Churches of the wider Anglican Communion, as held by those professing to stand within the Catholic tradition.

In furtherance of these aims and objectives, Affirming Catholicism is producing this series of booklets. The series will encompass two sets of books: one set will attempt to present a clear, well-argued Catholic viewpoint on issues of debate facing the Church at any given time; the other set will cover traditional doctrinal themes. The editor of the series is Jeffrey John; the other titles in the series are listed at the front of this booklet.

To order these publications individually or on subscription, or for enquiries regard-ing the aims and activities of Affirming Catholicism write to:

The Secretary
Mainstream
St Mary-le-Bow
Cheapside
London EC2V 6AU

Tel: 0171–329 4070

What is the Problem?

To most church people, 'folk religion' is a pretty derogatory term. Describing the beliefs which make up the religion of the mass of people outside the churchgoing community, it is often used to mark those beliefs as impure and inadequate, in contrast with the supposed completeness and purity of church religion. And so the christenings, weddings and funerals for which millions of people still look to the Christian Church (and especially to the Church of England) are implicitly emptied of much religious meaning. Folk religion, we are led to believe, is sentimental and undemanding, a black hole into which disappears the religious meaning not only of the rites of passage, but also of *Songs of Praise*, Remembrance Day, Christmas cribs and carols, Christingles, hot cross buns and Easter eggs.

This suspicion of folk religion is not without foundation. There has always been an ambiguous relationship between the 'official religion' of the Church and the religious beliefs and practices of the common people. Even when it has run in thoroughly conventional channels, popular piety has often been more expansively enthusiastic, and less sharply focused, than the teaching and ecclesiastical discipline articulated by the clergy. This was true as much of pilgrimages and relic cults in the Middle Ages as it is of some charismatic and healing movements today.

But the gap between popular belief and official religion remained generally unproblematic while the one Catholic Church held undisputed control of Christian identity in Britain, and Christianity was acknowledged as the religion of virtually all of the population. It was possible to assume uniformity of doctrine and practice; it was rarely necessary to impose it. The breaking of uniformity in the sixteenth and seventeenth centuries gave rise to denominational rivalry, and led to a crisis in the discipline of the established Church; nevertheless, mostly rivalries were contained within a recognizably 'orthodox' Christian framework. The problem of people presenting their children for baptism, for example, with scarcely any knowledge or understanding of the

Christian faith hardly arose in the way in which it does today. To all intents and purposes, the religion of the people still overlapped sufficiently with the official religion of the churches, for the tension between the two to pass largely unremarked.

That can hardly be said to be true today. A century of near continuous church decline has left churchgoing as an activity of a small minority of the population. Many of the means by which Christianity was taught to successive generations in the past have shrunk too. New opportunities for leisure and new working patterns, have altered the character of local communities, and destroyed the traditional idea of Sunday as a day of worship and rest. The spectrum of belief systems alternative to Christianity has widened enormously. For all these reasons, and many more, Christians must be more acutely aware than ever before of the extent to which their particular beliefs are *not* shared by a substantial proportion of the population.

So, in this Decade of Evangelism, there are a number of pressing questions to be asked. Exactly what is, today, 'folk religion'? Religiously speaking, in what kind of society do we now live? Given this context, whatever it may be, must we accept without question the simply derogatory view of folk religion common among many Christians? How are we to conceive of the mission of the Church in our society?

There are complex issues here. In this booklet I have adopted a selective approach, trying to develop an overall view of folk religion without getting bogged down in detailed discussion of specific trends in popular belief. I write as someone ministering to a mixed, inner-city parish, constantly bumping up against the vexed question of what relationship the Church of England now bears to the population at large, aware of the failure of our church to attract more than a small proportion of our parish, and yet surprised time and again by the extent to which non-churchgoers identify themselves as Christian and claim to support the work of the Church. I also write as one supportive of the objectives of Affirming Catholicism, and so I have one further question in mind: do we, as Anglican Catholics, have anything distinctive to offer the Church of England by way of an approach to the religious needs and perceptions of the non-churchgoing public?

The religion of the people

'Believing without Belonging'

Believing without Belonging is the subtitle of Grace Davie's recent survey of religion in contemporary Britain. Taking her cue from various polls and surveys of popular religious attitudes, Davie argues that the decline of church-going has not been paralleled by a decline in actual religious belief in the population at large. The 1990 European Values Study, for example, showed that some 71% of the population claimed to believe in God, some 68% in sin, and 64% in the soul; 54% would define themselves as religious people, and 53% claim to need special moments of prayer.[1] Active membership (variously defined) of Christian churches, however, is 14.4%, and regular churchgoing attracts under half of that figure.[2]

It is, of course, very difficult to assess to what extent the religious beliefs of those who do not attend church are in any sense 'Christian', or indeed how seriously they are taken by those who profess them. But, as Davie points out, the surveys do lead to a number of conclusions. Religious experience and belief of some kind remains important for a substantial majority of the British population. Even taking into account the existence of other faiths in this country, the historical context makes it highly probably that the religious beliefs of most people do overlap considerably with orthodox Christian belief. But these popular beliefs are not easily translated into active commitment to church attendance.

This much is well known, especially to Christian ministers who frequently have the experience of visiting non-churchgoing families in advance of, say, funerals, only to find it said of the deceased that they were good Christian people: 'Oh no she never went to church, but she was a good Christian; she would do anything for you.' Church of England clergy perhaps encounter this sort of reaction more often than others. If baptism is taken as the true mark of church membership, then it is still the case that almost half of the population of England may lay claim to identification as Anglican Christians.

Catholicism and Folk Religion · 3

Yet little over 5% of those baptized by Anglican clergy actually attend Anglican churches. Nationally the Church of England looks like one of its medieval cathedrals, a great and historic monument, frequented by millions of occasional visitors, used regularly by a mere handful.

What is it, then, about church life which fails to attract more than a small proportion of those who profess some form of Christian allegiance? It is not my purpose here to run through the whole range of possible answers to that question. But one thing does need to be said at the outset. Simplistic assertions about the 'secularization' of society in this context are not helpful. Undoubtedly there *is* a secularizing trend in some aspects of our national culture: evidence of this might be, for example, the continuing decline in the popularity of religious weddings and in baptism, the breakdown of national moral consensus on various sexual issues, and the increasingly controversial nature of religious education.

But against that could be set many other signs of resistance to secularization, and even of resurgence in religious belief. The continued high level of stated, personal belief in the population at large makes it very difficult to accept simple explanations based on 'secularization' at face value. Disasters in particular seem to call for expressions of grief and pain which are articulated in explicitly religious forms: Grace Davie dwells, for example, on the extraordinary scenes of mourning in the wake of the Hillsborough disaster.[3] There may be a sense in which some church leaders have taken on a much higher national profile in recent years, voicing concerns over government policy or social conditions, with some claim to speak for the conscience of the country as a whole. And there are, too, some growing churches, particularly at the evangelical end of the spectrum.

So we do not live in a 'secular' society, whatever that may mean. There is plenty of evidence to suggest that religion is alive, if not particularly well, in our society. Its power varies from area to area, from ethnic group to ethnic group, from age group to age group. Yet its relationship to church life is more uneasy, more problematic, than it has ever been.

Analyzing folk religion

Just what, then, does 'folk religion' consist of? For a start, we should note the beliefs and practices which surround the great events of life: birth, marriage and the establishment of sexual relationships, and death. It is no accident that these stages are marked, broadly, by the rites of passage, those Christian services which oversee each of these events. To these three we might add confirmation, with the popular belief that it is essentially an adolescent rite, marking the passage from childhood to youth.

All these stages are 'life-defining' in the sense that they signpost most obviously the journey of a person through time; they are the points at which personal experience intersects with the great mysteries of life. But they are also life-defining in the sense that they reflect and construct affective relationships, generally within the family. So they touch us in those two most personal aspects of our lives, our relationships with others and our own sense of identity and purpose.

Some defenders of a liberal and tolerant Church policy towards folk religion would leave the analysis of popular religious belief just about at this point. Through each of these rites it is possible, they would say, to explore a rich world of theological association which still exists to some extent in popular culture. Baptism, for example, undoubtedly can focus the sense of awe and mystery that parents feel at the creation of a new life; and into this sense of awe and mystery it is possible sometimes to read a similar awe at the creativity of God. Hence the lasting popularity of 'All things bright and beautiful' as a baptismal hymn, to the despair of clergy hoping to inject a bit of musical variety into the ceremony.

But an analysis of folk religion which stopped at this point would scarcely be satisfactory. First, it is impossible to determine the extent to which this 'rich world of theological association' really exists outside the wishful thinking of some clergy. Many people, when pressed, give no reason for approaching the church for one of these rites beyond the belief that it is the usual, traditional or 'normal' thing to do. The rites attract a huge range of beliefs, which at one end of the scale are no more than conventional or superstitious, and at the other shade into an acknowledged Christian pattern. So, even on these matters, folk religion would appear to be extremely fluid.

Second, to rely on these rites alone would seem to imply that most people have a form of inactive, largely dormant faith which is only awakened at certain great events in their lives. However, if modern surveys of religious belief establish anything without question, it is that a high proportion of people have beliefs which impinge upon their *everyday* lives – in that sense, they are *actively* religious. And that means that they have beliefs about prayer, about religious values, and about religious experience which cannot be subsumed under the rites of passage.

Exactly what these beliefs are is not easy to say. A belief in prayer would imply a belief that someone answers prayer, and so the idea of a God as a protective figure would seem to be common, with the corresponding idea that the course of our lives is not determined by us alone. The persistence of religious values would suggest that there is still a common feeling that there are certain things which God 'wants' us to do, and certain things he doesn't want us to do. But reaching a definite view of the content of these beliefs doesn't seem to be possible anymore, so great is their variety.

Third, we must beware of being beguiled by our own terminology. Neither the word 'folk' nor the word 'religion' themselves can carry us very far in trying to define popular religious belief. The word 'folk', used in this context, is essentially a Victorian concept, employed by ethnographers in a romanticized sense to distinguish what they believed to be the traditional values and customs of the common people from modern, artificial and (as they saw them) corrosive values. And again, try as we might, we cannot get away from the possibility that our use of the term 'religion' is defined largely by our own package of Christian beliefs, including our own perception of the importance of baptism, marriage and the funeral service. We take our understanding of what constitutes religion, and then go in search of something 'out there' in society at large to which it corresponds.

So the term 'folk religion' can be no more than a useful but limited working tool. The fluidity of popular belief is such that there is no social reality which the term can define and describe adequately, and we cannot give it firm, conceptual content. It is not, as such, a 'system' of belief. Its hallmarks at best are variety and flexibility. In this, folk religion simply echoes the pluralist character of modern society. But there are still Christian components in the religious beliefs of many people, and in the end it is surely from that basis that a positive assessment of popular belief must begin, rather than from the presupposition that folk religion represents a compact, alternative belief system.

Faith and understanding
If, so far in this booklet, folk religion has proved to be an extremely slippery concept, eluding any attempt to capture it by the fine net of analysis, still I have to say that there is yet more complexity, more slipperiness, to be inserted into the picture. Not only is it the case that popular religious belief exists to a considerable extent outside the domain of conventional church life, and that it is characterized by an extreme variety, but even where it is possible to identify Christian themes, it is by no means certain that we can expect to

find a uniform level of seriousness and understanding across the population at large.

You may find my use of the words 'seriousness' and 'understanding' here uncomfortable. You would be right to do so, for these words touch on one of the most profound but rarely acknowledged differences between those Christians who are broadly supportive of folk religion, and those who are highly critical of it. Critics of folk religion tend to have a highly dismissive attitude towards anything which cannot be openly and directly expressed as Christian belief. They tend to over-simplify non-Christian beliefs (as well, some might feel, as Christian ones), and mark them off sharply from the faith of the Church, coming dangerously near to denying the title 'Christian' to those who might claim it for themselves. They use pejorative terms such as 'pagan' and 'secular' too readily.

Defenders of folk religion, on the other hand, tend to fall too easily into the opposite trap, seizing on all sorts of different vestiges of Christian belief and practice as if these together added up to a profound but inarticulated religious faith. Once such a faith has been hypothesized, *any* degree of contact between Church and people would seem to be justified, whatever the actual beliefs of those individuals approaching the Church for its ministrations.

A concrete illustration, homing in on the issue of baptism, might make these two positions clearer. Let us suppose that Jack and Jill are two practising Anglican Christians who marry and have four sons, John, Paul, Ringo and George. All four are baptized as babies. John rejects Christianity in adolescence, moves in with his girlfriend (herself not a Christian), and they have children of their own. Paul never rejects Christianity directly, but church bores him, and he has little to do with it. Ringo likewise falls away from the church, but he does have quite strong personal religious beliefs, even if these contain some markedly 'new age' or 'pagan' features. Of the four, only George remains, eventually, a regular churchgoer.

Now let us suppose that all four have children of their own. Whose children should we allow to be baptized? At first glance, this is an easy question, depending on your point of view. An uncritical appreciator of folk religion would probably say 'All of them', if, that is, they are prepared, at least, to say the words required of them in the baptism liturgy. A critic would also like to say 'All of them', but there would have to be substantial signs of growth in faith on the part of Paul and Ringo (I'm leaving aside, for the sake of clarity, their partners), and a complete revolution in faith on the part of John, before they could even begin to be considered. And, further, the critic would be unlikely to be satisfied until *all four* are able to profess faith coherently enough to make it certain that they understand what it is they are affirming and promising in the baptismal liturgy.

Both of these positions are based on an overly simplistic view of the way we come to faith. To pretend that folk religion is such that no exploration and test of faith is necessary at all is to pretend that it is what it is demonstrably not – a coherent system of beliefs which can be slotted comfortably into the existing pattern of Church practice. On the other hand, to claim that anything short of a fully articulated and fully understood faith is inadequate is to assume that there is a fixed, minimal condition which all Christians must meet before they can claim the title for themselves.

It is surely evident at once that human beings simply do not work like this. We all grow in faith, beginning often at a point of near incomprehension about our beliefs, and building our experiences of God in prayer, in our lives and in our relationships with other people into our growing understanding of ourselves and of our faith. In that sense, there is a multiplicity of different levels of understanding of the Christian faith even within the community of regular churchgoers. To pretend otherwise would be to suppose, by implication, that the mentally impaired and the young cannot be Christians in the same sense as others can.

That multiplicity exists even within ourselves. When I say the Nicene Creed every Sunday, I cannot in all honesty claim that I understand every article of the creed to the same degree and in exactly the same way, or indeed that any doubts I may have on each of them have equally been laid to rest. The point is that I assent to them, and the search for God which my faith attempts to encapsulate is based on the creed, and the creed stands as a symbol of the faith of the Church into which I am included by my baptism. Now I am not trying to pretend that the multiplicity of belief in itself is an argument for affirming as Christians those who may not see themselves as such. But it does demonstrate the fallacy of thinking that we can draw a very sharp dividing line between Christian and 'non-Christian' lives.

The key question, returning to my example of the four fathers, is not so much about what people know as about the way they see their lives. Instead of pretending that all four have already accepted the key elements of the Christian faith, or instead of requiring them to be able to give an account of faith which will cover all those key elements, in effect we should be saying to them 'Will you acknowledge this as the basis on which you will try to lead your life?' Assent to *that* is the determining point at which we should be able to welcome families in baptism. And the readiness of parents or candidates to make that acknowledgement should be matched, on our part, by a recognition that the beliefs and values they already confess may well take them a long way towards 'understanding' the deeper mysteries of the Christian faith.

So the variety and flexibility of popular belief, its multiplicity, as I have called it, does not necessarily put it at a great distance from the faith and practice of the Church. Instead of thinking in terms of two mutually opposed sets of beliefs, those of the visible Church, and those of the world outside the Church, perhaps we should recognize a continuum of values and beliefs, many of which are held by people who never actually attend church. Far from inhabiting a splendid isolation, the Church in this country does have many roots outside its own visible organization, roots stretching out into the seemingly arid territory of folk religion.

The Church of England and the people

The myth of Anglican comprehensiveness
Now that I have given some account of the concept of folk religion and what it entails, even if it has ended up looking more open-ended and featureless than you might originally have imagined it to be, I want to look at the Church of England, in order to clarify its relationship with this extremely diffuse cluster of beliefs and values. My aim is not to attempt to delineate Anglican theology, or even to construct an ecclesiology, but simply to try to identify what the Church of England looks like from the point of view of popular belief.

First of all, then, it would be as well to deal with the idea of Anglican comprehensiveness, an idea which continues to delude many Anglicans into thinking that their church is more open to non-churchgoers than other churches are. The idea of comprehensiveness is an attractive one: it is a residue of the once compelling Anglican claim to minister to the spiritual needs of the vast majority of the population, though for centuries this claim was not interpreted in the same way as our modern idea of comprehensiveness would imply. In the modern sense, it is usually taken to mean a tolerance of widely different theologies under the umbrella of one ecclesial system.

Now it is not to the point that diversity actually exists within the Church of England. In making demands at all of its members, a church must create some tensions between itself and the society in which it exists. When someone approaches an Anglican church for the first time, their view of the Church of England is likely to be formed by their experience of that particular encounter, not by a theory of comprehensiveness. And it is undoubtedly true that a large number of Anglican churches do not embody in practice the comprehensiveness they claim in theory. Nor could it be otherwise; they have distinctive doctrines which support distinctive liturgical practices, they rely on particular networks of people, they identify with particular values and social groups; in all these ways they must exclude as well as include.

The parochial system itself does not make comprehensiveness much more of a reality, either. Certainly in our towns and cities parish boundaries are generally not of much significance to the non-churchgoing public. If they identify at all with a particular church, it is most likely to be for family and geographical reasons. 'Their' church is the one they were baptized in, or the one their parents were married in, or the one just round the corner. From this perspective, doctrinal and even denominational identities can be extremely blurred.

And if what little sense of church identity that does exist is structured largely in this local and family-centred way, then the sense of shock and rebuff when the church does refuse its ministrations for some reason, or attempt to require firm commitment, naturally enough will be considerable. As I have already implied, and will go on to argue, the Church must make demands and impose some boundaries. The claimed 'comprehensiveness' of the Church of England is of little help, then, in attempting to describe how the Church is perceived in popular belief.

Establishment, the Press, nationalism and division
Having disposed of comprehensiveness, I should deal with three further aspects of the Church of England which could have a bearing on my argument. One, naturally enough, is the question of Establishment, and in particular the status of the Church of England as the religion of the monarch and the official religion of the State. Another is the related but distinct question of Anglicanism and national identity. Finally, there is the question of the treatment of the Church of England in the media.

The fact that the Church of England is an established Church clearly has had a major impact on its popular perception. In their role as registrars, for example, parish priests have an important local position as functionaries for registering (and so for holding) weddings. In a more general sense, Establishment undoubtedly has a role in maintaining a high public profile for the Church of England, especially at the annual Remembrance Day services and similar occasions. And there are other instances of influence and status which flow from Establishment, such as the position of chaplaincies to hospitals, prisons and other institutions. But there are reasons for thinking that the real impact of Establishment is on the wane. Church weddings are in decline. Growing ecumenical sensitivities have meant that representatives of other Christian denominations have begun to match Anglican chaplains in their work.

And then there is the question of the monarchy. The recent furore caused by the Prince of Wales' suggestion that, were he to become monarch, he would like to be seen as 'Defender of faith' rather than as 'Defender of the Faith' led to some interesting and unexpected consequences, such as the way in which some Muslim leaders spoke up for the idea of an established Church. But there is not much evidence that the status of the reigning monarch as 'Supreme Governor' of the Church of England is widely known and understood by the population at large, or that it influences people to identify with Anglicanism who might not otherwise do so.

In the past, one of the principal justifications for Establishment was the concept of national identity. The Church of England was the Catholic Church *in England*, and there was an assumed link between English national character, English political and social institutions, and the Church. Whatever weight that view once had has largely disappeared. Once again, church decline, the relative prominence of other denominations (especially the Roman Catholic Church), and the growth of ethnic minorities have all made the 'Englishness' of the Anglican Church an irrelevance. What has not been lost, of course, is the historical baggage that once accompanied such a claim. The historic churches and cathedrals remain, and though in settled rural communities there may still be a widespread feeling that the church does indeed stand for something timeless, of a piece with the people and landscape, in most other social contexts the Church is in danger of being seen as just another facet of the heritage industry.

Media images may or may not tell us something about popular views of the Church. The cumulative effect of 'Vicars and knickers' stories in the tabloids, traced weekly by Paul Handley in the *Church Times*, must surely be damaging for the Church, but more positive images and stories are hard to find and rarely say very much about what people really think and experience of the Church. Mostly these images focus on the character and work of the clergy themselves, and scarcely address the more fundamental questions of Christian faith. They present the clergy, unsurprisingly, as well-intentioned, a bit muddled and generally ineffectual. Even when, as with the television programme *The Vicar of Dibley*, a rather different character is featured, still the general context of the programme is one of nostalgic, rural, eccentric charm, a far cry from the reality of the vast majority of Anglican parishes.

The multi-faceted nature of folk religion means that it is impossible to rule out altogether the possibility that each of the various images of the Church of England I have described so far does have some resonance still in popular belief. But none of them appears to take us very far along the road of identifying the Church of England from a popular perspective. Other views could be taken into account, especially those of the Church as predominantly white, middle class and conservative, though again it would be very difficult to assess how much weight should be given to them.

Alongside all these various images of the Church of England is a countervailing impression, gradually receiving more attention publicly, of the Church as a seriously divided institution. Division receives public attention because, as a Catholic journalist recently reminded us, 'Conflict is a key ingredient in news'.[4] Catholic Anglicans could not help but be aware of the extent of these divisions. The Church of England does not in practice conform to the uniform picture of its own mythology, or of constitutional theory. It contains within itself groups of Christians whose theologies differ so greatly that some of us wonder how it has ever managed to keep together. An overarching Anglican ecclesiology capable of uniting this theological diversity has proved to be elusive so far, even though, *pace* Stephen Sykes, we may accept that the possibility of such an ecclesiology is one we cannot afford to let go.[5] Why else be Anglican? Yet the divisions demonstrate that there is no easy option with regard to folk religion. We cannot reach a picture of the Church of England which will encapsulate the aspirations and spiritual needs of all of our people, not only because those aspirations and needs themselves are so diverse, but because the Church's regular members are so diverse too.

The religion of Catholicism

Catholic life

So far, I have presented mainly a negative case. I have tried to give a flavour of the range and diversity of folk religion, but I have resisted the suggestion that there are leading features of it which can be wrapped up into a compact system of belief. In turn, I have tried to show that a number of ways in which the Church of England is commonly seen, neither reflect adequately the reality of the contemporary Church, nor offer by implication a firm basis for rapprochement between the Church and the unchurched. But I have not taken this line because I have a negative view of the current prospects and situation of the Church of England. It is because I believe that the Church must find justification for its own distinctive practice from within the traditional resources of Christianity: we cannot afford to suppose any longer that there is a distinctive English, national, religious character which the Church of England can reflect and articulate. Anglican Catholics might expect, then, to find from within their own identity and practice some clues as to how the gap between Church and people may be bridged.

The Catholic idea of the Church is one which can embrace considerable diversity in local liturgical and ecclesial practice. Catholicism, Christopher Irvine tells us, is in essence 'a living sense of being a part of the universal Church'.[6] Diversity is possible because the unity of the Church transcends the practice of individual churches. It is an ecclesial unity drawn together in the bishop, and through him in continuity with the Church in history.

Furthermore, the idea of the Church as the whole body of the faithful, whose faith is articulated in the traditional credal formularies of the Church, implies that the inability of an individual to give an account of his or her faith does not thereby deny to them the title 'Christian'. This is perhaps one of the most striking differences between Catholic and Evangelical interpretations of faith, and it is one of the principal reasons why Catholics are able so often to affirm faith where others may be blind to it. It is expressed forcefully by the French Roman Catholic, Henri de Lubac, citing an unnamed source: ' "Confession of faith in the creed is always made in the name of the whole Church"; that is why someone who has no more than an "unformed" faith can still truly say that he believes'.[7]

This ecclesiology, which is inclusive because it is not dependent on the faith of individual believers, is matched in the implications of sacramental theology. For the force of the sacrament, signifying and imparting grace, is not dependent finally on the individual's purity of faith. It derives principally from the Church's faithfulness to its historic mission, in which scripture and tradition provide the sources and norms, and from its continuity with the church of the apostles. When properly administered, the sacraments are inclusive because they cannot be changed, adapted, or manipulated by individuals; they stand over and against the wilfulness of human beings. And so it is a characteristic emphasis of writers in the Catholic tradition that the sacraments are anti-egoistical, anti-individualistic, egalitarian. For this very reason, Newman pointed out, confirmation should be administered when the young are still under some form of constraint, before they have 'wilfully sinned in any gross way'.[8] Michael Ramsey, similarly, described how, in the eucharist, the Christian 'shares in the death once died and finds his life no longer his own but united with Christ and with the people of God'.[9] I like especially the language of the Anglican Catholic socialist, Stewart Headlam, who described baptism as 'the sacrament of equality' and communion as 'the sacrament of brotherhood' (or fraternity).[10]

All this accords very well with the incarnational nature of our faith. The humanity assumed by the Son of God universalizes the potential of all humankind for redemption. It follows that there is a sense in which all of us, made in the image of God, are equally brought before God in Christ, and so 'the true light, which enlightens everyone' (John 1.10) may be experienced in quite unexpected ways, or seen in quite unexpected encounters with people who have little or no contact with the Christian Church. Indeed such is the force of this argument, which of course does not exclusively belong within the Catholic 'wing' of Christianity, but which does have a special place and strength within Catholic theology, that some people have based an entire case for affirming folk religion on this ground alone. But there is a good reason why incarnational theology carries us only so far in an attempt to reach a more appreciative view of folk religion, and that is because the perception that God is present in many unforeseen situations does not enable us to determine for ourselves *how* and *where* he is present. It does not get us off the hook of having to negotiate a critical encounter with popular belief. Moreover, simply to use incarnational theology as a justification for uncritically affirming folk religion would do little justice to the human need for redemption. Anyone tempted to go down that road should look a little more closely at the meditation on the tensions between discipleship and the world in the seventeenth chapter of John's gospel.

Catholic ecclesiology and theology in turn can encourage characteristic ways of worship and teaching which can draw into the Church the wide diversity of different abilities and backgrounds to be found in the population at large. There is, for example, the power of symbolism. In another booklet in this series, Christopher Irvine has drawn attention to the potential of the sacramental symbol not only to engender a 'wide range of associations and responses', but to 'create new possibilities for human existence and to depict deeper realities.'[11] Sacramental symbolism is by far the most potent answer Catholic Anglicans can provide to what Irvine dubs the 'crisis of symbolism' in our society, the sense in which the language of symbols has become 'a forgotten language' in our culture.[12] By its saturation in Christian history and tradition the Catholic movement possesses immediate access to a whole range of ritual gestures and symbolic actions which may both express aspects of Christian truth and bridge the gap between church practice and popular culture. The sharing of meals, the giving of gifts, acts and gestures of reconciliation, these are just some of the ways in which the Church may be able to sacralize the stuff of human experience.

In a recent study of evangelism, the Evangelical writer John Drane has admitted the force of many criticisms of conventional Evangelical language for conversion, and argued instead (thus moving unconsciously nearer to a Catholic position) that conversion is a process of many events.[13] That view of conversion as process (I had much rather use the vocabulary of growth and journey) demonstrates the realism of Catholic approaches to the teaching office of the Church. Holding fully to its dogmatic responsibilities, these approaches have tended to emphasize the prior importance of participation in the life of the Church. This accords fully with my earlier assertion that Christian faith, first and foremost, involves a certain frame of mind – a commitment to living life in a certain way – rather than to achieving a certain level of knowledge. Knowledge of doctrine, and the ability to give a consistent, verbal account of conversion and faith are not, in the Catholic view, prior conditions required of individual believers. Often, it is true, this emphasis has encouraged slovenly teaching on the party of clergy, or a neglect of the teaching office altogether. But its advantage has been its flexibility, its readiness to adapt its methods to suit the temperament and abilities of believers themselves. Early Tractarian theology articulated this emphasis through what was called the doctrine of reserve. In two of the *Tracts for the Times*, Isaac Williams argued that religious truth should be communicated to believers only as and when they were morally fit to receive it. Williams's arguments were seized on by critics, including many Evangelical clergy, as evidence of Tractarian duplicity, since they implied that elements of Christian truth should be withheld from would-be believers. But Williams did no more than assume an elementary truth of religious psychology, that the fullness of Christian belief could not be grasped at one go, but required growth in personal spirituality. The doctrine of reserve represented, then, a refusal to drive a wedge between knowledge of God and moral worth, a refusal consistent with the oldest traditions of mystical theology.

In a way, it is not surprising that my discussion of themes in Catholicism has found its way back to the issue of the basis on which religious faith is held. I could have called in my defence the work of James Fowler and others on 'Stages of Faith'.[14] But the Catholic insight that participation in the life of faith, with the commitment that that involves, precedes the intellectual processes of understanding and articulating the doctrines of the faith, and must inform them, seems to me strong enough to need no support from other quarters. To the extreme diversity of popular belief, this Catholic understanding should be able to respond positively at whatever level first approaches to the Church are made.

And yet nagging questions remain. Is there not a danger here of building the house of faith on the shifting sands of folk religion? Or, if you prefer a less clichéd way of putting it, doesn't the seeming priority here of belonging over believing actually do an injustice to the content of revealed truth? And further, doesn't it conflict directly with what Grace Davie takes as the key characteristic of folk religion itself, that is the condition of believing without belonging? I shall try to address both of these questions in the next two sections.

Gospel imperatives
The persuasiveness of many Evangelical critiques of current Church practice in part derives from their apparent readiness to set biblical insights at the very centre of their theology of the Church. Without prejudging the results of critical exegesis of scripture, and without displacing those other legs of

the Catholic interpretation of authority, tradition and reason, it is still hard to escape the conclusion that church practice must be driven by biblical insights, if not by biblical models. This is fully in accord with Stephen Sykes' repetition that 'Anglicans are right to insist that we should under no circumstances lose contact with the biblical witness to the Church in its full historic reality.'[15]

So Catholic Anglicans have nothing to lose from this emphasis on the imperatives of the gospel. But the Catholic insistence that the authority of scripture must be mediated through the tradition of the Church, and that there is a continuous thread of apostolic authority from the first century to this which defines the very being of the Catholic and Apostolic Church, frequently tends to lead in a very different direction from that pointed out by Evangelical Protestantism. Might not Catholic responses to folk religion represent just such a divergence?

We can see how such a criticism could be made by looking once again at the example of baptism. Colin Buchanan has set out very clearly what he claims to be the biblical doctrine of baptism, summed up in two 'biblical principles': first, 'submission to baptism is nothing other than submission to the gospel, and submission to the gospel is expressed and consummated in submission to baptism'; and second, 'baptism gives a sharp edge to the visible Church'. Together, he asserts, these two principles show that baptism 'symbolizes and portrays God's saving love given and *received*'.[16] If, for the sake of argument, we were to take this as a satisfactory statement of the New Testament view, it would seem to be very easy to attack what frequently passes for Catholic baptismal practice. In relatively few Catholic parishes is evidence required of parents (for example, by way of regular church attendance) to show that they have indeed 'submitted' to the gospel; a very high proportion of parents fail to bring their children along to Sunday school, or to church, or in time to confirmation; altogether the 'sharp edge' between the visible Church and the world appears to be lacking. Here, if anywhere, the accusation that Catholicism tends to suppress the hard demands of the gospel in favour of easy accommodation with the world would seem to be justified.

But is that really the case? Neither of Buchanan's biblical principles actually need be contradicted in most cases of baptism in Anglican churches. If religious faith is above all a commitment to see life a certain way, then 'submission to the gospel' may be shown in many different ways, and the lack of subsequent evidence for growth in faith is not in itself a sign that that submission initially has not taken place. When parents identify themselves as Christians, and are prepared to make the affirmations and promises required of them, it would be an addition to what little we know of New Testament baptismal practice to put conditions on them in order to get them to demonstrate that they have indeed 'submitted'. If, as Buchanan himself points out, the silences of scripture are legion, then they are eloquent here on the whole question of how the Church should judge pre- and post-baptismal behaviour. Furthermore, it is the act of baptism itself, and what it says about the recipient of baptismal grace, which represents the 'sharp edge' between the visible Church and the world, not some notional level marking the supposed behaviour of baptismal candidates. Certainly, repentance of sin must, on the biblical view, precede baptism, but how that is demonstrated is nowhere set out.

Once again, I have not set out to challenge Buchanan's biblical case directly. All I have tried to show is that even his version of the biblical case cannot on its own serve as a sufficient basis for a critique of much current baptismal practice. Except in those rare cases where parents actually repudiate Christian belief, denying that they wish to pursue a life of faith, there is nothing to suggest any criteria we could use by which the adequacy of the faith of candidates and their parents can be judged. Catholic practice, in that sense, may be fully consonant with Buchanan's own biblical perspective.

But my aim is not to work over the theology and practice of baptism as such. The example of baptism merely helps us to see how some current Catholic practice need not involve a repudiation or partial suppression of gospel principles. But the argument, of course, must be put in a stronger form than that. The biblical insights are foundational, and the appeal to tradition does not contradict or supplement the primacy of the biblical revelation, but rather enables us to see how the biblical witness has been received and followed by the community of the faithful. No wedge should be driven between tradition and the imperatives of the gospel; on the Catholic view, these are both aspects of one reality.

And so, from this standpoint, we can be wary of approaches to folk religion which are based on a policy of accommodation, suppressing the demands Christianity undoubtedly places on its followers in order to draw in as many people as possible. Instead, a Church confident of itself and of its historic mission to 'make disciples of all the nations' (Matthew 28.19) can afford to be critical of much which passes for contemporary belief. The policy to follow is one of "retrieval" by which those popular beliefs and insights which are consonant with the faith of the Church can act as points of contact.

The acknowledgement that the faith of the Church must be grounded in the scriptural revelation is exactly what underlines the traditional Catholic emphasis on the importance of dogma. For the creeds and the dogmatic formulae of the Church seek to articulate the faith to which scripture points us. Ramsey, again, brought this out most clearly:

[Since] Truth and life and worship are inseparable, the scriptures and the Creeds are not given for use in isolation. They form, with the ministry and the sacraments, one close-knit structure which points the Christians to the historical facts wherein God is revealed, and to the life and experience of the universal society.[17]

The growth and the very life of the Christian community are closely bound up with the extent to which the faith of the Church is prayed, taught, learnt and lived out in the lives of its members. It can never be simply a passive thing.

It is the proclamation of the gospel in this global sense which enables Catholic Anglicans to hold both to the foundational quality and authority of the biblical witness and to the primarily 'lived' rather than 'learned' nature of religious faith. It requires us not to place too much trust in our own standards and tests of the quality of faith of people – standards and tests which may come dangerously near to a form of idolatry – but instead to put the proclamation of the Truth at the centre of our church practice. In the case of baptism, for example, this approach would shift the onus of baptismal policy from assessing the quality of an individual's faith to the responsibility of the Church for making the truth and meaning of the gospel clear to those who approach us in terms that they can grasp.

The case of baptism throws light on the whole question of the relationship between the Church and folk religion. If we are ready to take people seriously who call themselves Christians when they approach the church for baptism, and to work with the level of faith they possess, then we are likely to acknowledge the sincerity of the faith of many of the unchurched, and indeed the real insights into religious truth which they may possess. But that readiness, on the part of a Church whole-heartedly committed to its evangelical mission, would certainly not mean a spirit of easy capitulation to the values of the world at large.

Difficulties and discontinuities

I can't pretend that I have disposed of all of the difficulties my argument might raise. I have tried to demonstrate how the historic resources of Catholic

Anglicanism might be used to reach a more positive and appreciative view of much that passes for folk religion, without compromising the Church's hold on truth. I have tried do so by reversing the common approach to this subject, looking not for shards of light and faith outside the Church on the presupposition that God is at work in the world (though this is a presupposition I share), but for an understanding of Christian faith and life which accords fully with scripture and tradition and yet is sufficiently rich and broad to include a wide range of different human responses to the gospel. But difficulties do remain. I have already touched slightly on one, the practical difficulty of implementing a baptismal policy which is firm on teaching and yet still in another sense unconditional. Here I want to raise what I believe to be the more serious remaining difficulties.

If, as Grace Davie has it, folk religion is marked by believing without belonging, then the Catholic tendency to reverse that order may represent a real discontinuity with popular belief. How do you generate a sense of belonging? It is clearly an implication of Davie's analysis – and one backed up by various historical studies – that the persistence of Christian forms of belief stands beside powerful anti-clerical, or at least anti-Church perceptions.[18] These are difficult perceptions to overcome. That they *can* be overcome is demonstrated by the remarkable story of Father David Diamond, Rector of St Paul's, Deptford for twenty-three years until his death in 1992.[19] Fr Diamond simply ignored conventional modern advice about moving away from reliance on the building and reducing overt signs of clericalism such as distinctive dress. He left his church open at all times, spent lavishly on its restoration, and built it up again as a sign of the vibrancy of Deptford life. Through the Deptford Festival he drew thousands to the church. There was a cost in all of this, to his health, amongst other things. And it is not by any means clear how lasting his ministry was in the sense of making new committed, churchgoing Christians. I don't want to hold him up, then, as a model. But his work does show that the discontinuity of Catholicism and folk religion need not be a crippling one. The persistence of Christian belief, albeit in a diffuse and sometimes superficial form, does mean that at the same time there is still a widespread sympathy and goodwill for the work of the Church.

Nevertheless, a further serious discontinuity emerges out of all of this. I have played down, deliberately, the importance of the rites of passage to some extent in my discussion of popular belief, though I can't escape the fact that these are still by far our most important points of contact with the unchurched. But there is one sacrament which is acknowledged by all

Anglicans, and yet which does not easily fit into the rhythms of life marked by the rites of passage. I mean, of course, the eucharist. The centrality of eucharistic worship in Catholic Anglicanism does not easily find an echo in the lives of the unchurched, except in the symbolic sense that the eucharist is a shared meal; and yet the first-time experience of the eucharist for the unchurched almost certainly is nothing like the conviviality of a meal. Part of the rationale for parish communion, pioneered by the likes of Gabriel Hebert and Henry de Candole, was that it sums up and expresses the unity of the worshipping community, and that does imply that there ought to be some relation between that sense of unity and the wider community of the parish. And yet in so many Anglican parishes today that sense of consolidated, traditional community has almost disappeared, and the disjuncture between church life and society at large has become very wide. Writing from what appears to me to be a standpoint wholly at odds with the meaning of communion, the journalist Ted Harrison nevertheless has captured this disjuncture by contrasting individual spiritual experience with corporate worship in the eucharist:

> The introduction of the parish Eucharist as the main service of the week is all part of the trend away from individuals seeking a spiritual experience in their own way to requiring of them a public Christian commitment. The more that such requirements are made, the less likely are these people to come to church even though they are seeking a spiritual experience.[20]

For Catholic Anglicans it is the Eucharist, and not baptism, which is the likeliest point of tension with folk religion, for it is precisely the eucharist which recreates and expresses our inner unity as the body of Christ, and as such it is and must be a direct challenge to the kind of individualism Harrison exalts. It is a point on which compromise does not seem possible, since to be a Christian is to be in relation with others, and the Church cannot exist as a mere collection of individuals seeking 'spiritual experiences'. The kind of superstitious approach to the sacrament which would see it as something I should receive for my benefit alone, as making 'my' communion, is a tempting way out of this dilemma, but one which falls sadly on the individualistic side.

The fact that there is a discontinuity here may be something with which we just have to live. As I have argued, there are very good reasons why we should be wary of building our church practice on folk religion: popular belief is not itself a compact system of values, and anyway our guiding norms and sources call us to values and beliefs which often contradict those held more widely in the world around us. It may be, again, that in expressing the inner unity of the Church, it is the eucharist which calls us to challenge divisive forces at work in our society: there may be a special place here for the teaching work of the Church. All this simply underlines the urgent need for a realism which recognizes the persistence of Christian belief among the unchurched, and seeks to reclaim them for the Church.

Reclaiming the secular

Strengths and weaknesses

Folk religion is an extremely shifting and indefinable phenomenon. It is not surprising that, in trying to reach some view of its relationship to the Church of England, I have had to cut across a number of other subject areas and controversies, some of which are treated in detail in other booklets in this series. The question of Establishment, for example, comes into the picture, as does sacramental theology, as does the question of church decline and its causes. An already complex picture would be complicated still further if, as rightly I should, I were to go on to discuss the variety of other issues which straddle the field: the persistence of racial and sexual prejudice in society at large and in the Church, the growth of other faith communities in this country, and contemporary manifestations of cultural identities (especially the 'heritage' industry), to name but a few.

It is partly because folk religion is not a definable 'thing' that I have taken the view that the most realistic course of action for the Church is one guided by a policy of 'retrieval' rather than a policy of accommodation. I have tried to say that we must have confidence in what we believe as Christians, first and foremost, before we can even begin to see where popular belief may still leave open paths of communication between Church and people. I have not thereby ruled out altogether the view that people experience God in many different ways, many of which do not fall remotely within the practical sphere of the activity of the Church. But, whilst I find that view attractive, it does not seem possible to find a common basis on which we can recognize or validate authentic experiences of God, unless that basis is found within the life of faith. So, as the use of the word 'Catholic' implies, in our work as church members there is an obligation on us to draw the outer limits of this life of faith as widely as possible, while still holding to the claim that it is a life which is sharply defined against many of the values and aspects of our world.

The strengths of the Catholic movement in the Church of England lie in its readiness to embrace the whole richess and diversity of the lives of the faithful, and, through sacramental theology and Catholic liturgical practice, its ability to find ways of recognizing and giving expression to the different stages of faith which individual believers have reached. In it the unchurched may find that their discomfort with the conventional vocabulary of Christian belief, and their confusion and uncertainty about particular dogmatic claims, need not bar them from full inclusion and participation in church life.

But the weaknesses of the Catholic movement are notorious, and can be found in so many parishes where the church has turned in on itself. Symbolism and ritual can become frozen, arcane and élitist, a positive barrier to evangelism. A high concept of the Church can be corrupted into a suffocating churchiness. A conviction of the possession of truth can become complacency, and a refusal to search for the signs of faith amongst those who are not churchgoers. In all these ways, far from being truly inclusive and universal, Catholicism can become sectarian and divisive, and often has become so.

Despite all this, in the Catholic tradition there is a real alternative to the two strategies of outright rejection and uncritical acceptance which bedevil Church attitudes to folk religion. A policy of 'retrieval' seeks to be true both to the integrity of the Church's historic mission, through an emphasis on teaching, and to the multiple ways in which believers understand the Church, through a view of faith as lived rather than learned. This alternative is not simply a *via media*, borrowing assertions and denials selectively from both sides. Theologically it draws on both the 'immanent' conception of God (as working through the lives of all people) and the 'transcendental' emphasis on the special revelation given in Christ, witnessed in scripture and interpreted by the Church. But it doesn't see these as essentially separate insights which somehow have to be cemented together: they are integrally related, joints aspects of the one reality which is the Church as the body of Christ. They are, admittedly, held in tension, and there is always the danger that the tension will break one way or the other. But tension is the mark of constructive, critical engagement, and the overlap between the religion of the people and the religion of the Church cannot be extended or amplified without it.

A changing world
It would be absurd to pretend that folk religion, the Church of England and Catholic tradition all exist in timeless form. My argument is written quite consciously from the perspective of the mid-1990s. It would be possible to

draw a very different picture of the relationship between the Church and popular belief by taking a snapshot from a different period of history. Go back one hundred and fifty years, for example, and you would find yourself in a situation in which levels of churchgoing were far higher than they are today, in which non-Christian religious traditions were almost non-existent in Britain, in which contacts with the unchurched were far more frequent and reached much further than they do today, and yet in which the Catholic tradition in the Church of England was regarded widely with suspicion and sometimes with open hostility.

At most, my argument would seem to imply that there are certain resources and insights within the Catholic tradition which may enable it successfully to build bridges to the unchurched, and that this is so because folk religion is such in this country *at this time* that it still contains a degree of sympathy with the Church which is surprising to those of us encountering it in our daily ministry. But we can't assume that this will always be the case. Popular belief is not static. There are signs that even the diffuse religious belief of a large proportion of the population is on the wane, and that this is true particularly amongst the young. Even if many young people eventually return to some form of faith, still we may be facing overall a generational collapse in Christian identity in years to come. The growth of 'new age' beliefs may continue, and may be a sign of a consumerism and syncretism in popular belief which would mark an even sharper divergence from orthodox Christianity. It may be, too, that further developments in the technology of communication will undermine the networks of personal association on which church life tends to thrive, and will prompt new forms of associations to which the Church will need to respond. These factors, and many others, suggest that folk religion in some ways will be very different in the future.

There is an element of urgency, then, about this question. If the Catholic wing of the Church of England does have a distinctive contribution to make in this Decade of Evangelism, both to the mission of the Church of England in particular, as well as to Christianity in general, there many not be much time left before existing chances of building on long-established cultural and social identities seep away. Were that to happen, that would not itself signify an end either to the Church of England's task of evangelism, or to the existence within it of the Catholic movement. However, knowing all we do about the overwhelming tendency of new churchgoers to come from those who already have some contact with existing churchgoers and some familiarity with religious faith, it would amount to a colossal loss of opportunity. It might also reflect a loss of nerve on the part of Catholic Anglicans, and a failure on their part to realize in practice the historic resources of their tradition.

Notes

1 G. Davie, *Religion in Britain since 1945: Believing without Belonging* (1994), p. 78.

2 *Op. cit.*, p. 46.

3 *Op. cit.*, pp. 88–91.

4 P. Vallely, *'The media, The Church, and the Truth'*, *Priests and People*, May, 1994, p. 175.

5 S. Sykes, *'Foundations of an Anglican Ecclesiology'*, in J. John (ed.), *Living the Mystery* (1994).

6 C. Irvine, *Worship, Church and Society* (1993), p. 35.

7 H. de Lubac, *The Splendour of the Church* (New ed., 1979), p. 23.

8 J. H. Newman, *Parochial and Plain Sermons* (New ed., 1869), Vol. 4, p. 63.

9 A M. Ramsey, *The Gospel and the Catholic Church* (1936), p. 118.

10 S. D. Headlam, *Christian Socialism: A Lecture* (1892), p. 7.

11 C. Irvine, *Making Present: The Practice of Catholic Life and Liturgy* (1994), p. 16.

12 *Op cit.*, p. 8.

13 J. Drane, *Evangelism for a New Age* (1994), ch. 4, 'What is Conversion?'

14 J. W. Fowler, *Stages of Faith* (1981).

15 Sykes, *op. cit.*, p. 39.

16 C. Buchanan, *Infant Baptism and the Gospel: the Church of England's Dilemma* (1993), p. 32.

17 Ramsey, *op. cit.*, p. 127.

18 See, for example, D. H. McLeod, *Religion and the People of Western Europe 1789–1970* (1981).

[19] R. Bomford and H. Potter (eds.), *Father Diamond of Deptford* (1994).

[20] E. Harrison, *Members Only: Is the Church becoming too exclusive?* (1994), p. 39.